# Fear is My Friend

*Expanding Astute Revelations!*

Robert Wilson

Editing by Amy Lignor

Copyright © 2012 Freedom of Speech Publishing, Inc.

All rights reserved.

ISBN: 1938634284
ISBN-13: 978-1-938634-28-4

# DEDICATION

This book is dedicated to my Mom Hazel Wilson and My Late Dad John Wilson.

# Fear is My Friend
## By Robert A. Wilson

For more books like this one, visit Robert A. Wilson's website at:
http://cowboy-wisdom.com/
2012 copyright by Freedom of Speech Publishing, Inc.
All rights reserved. No part of this book may be reproduced, distributed, or transmitted in any form or by any means, without permission in writing from the publisher.

Printed in the United States of America
The publisher offers discounts on this book when ordered in bulk quantities. For more information, contact Sales Department, Phone 815-290-9605, Email:
sales@FreedomOfSpeechPublishing.com

Product and company names mentioned herein are the trademarks or registered trademarks of their respective owners.

Freedom of Speech Publishing, Leawood KS, 66224
www.FreedomOfSpeechPublishing.com
ISBN: 1938634284
ISBN-13: 978-1-938634-28-4

# A SPECIAL THANK YOU TO YOU!

On behalf of everyone at Freedom Of Speech Publishing, thank you for choosing Fear is My Friend for your reading enjoyment.

As an added bonus and special thank you, for purchasing Fear is My Friend, you can enjoy discounts and special promotions on other Freedom of Speech Publishing products. Visit www.freedomeofspeech.com/vip to learn more.

We are committed to providing you with the highest level of customer satisfaction possible. If for any reason you have questions or comments, we are delighted to hear from you. Email us at cs@freedomofspeechpublishing.com or visit our website at: http://freedomofspeechpublishing.com/contact-us-2/.

If you enjoyed Fear is My Friend, visit www.freedomofspeechpublishing.com for a list of similar books or upcoming books.

Again, thank you for your patronage. We look forward to providing you more entertainment in the future.

# Contents

Author's Note ............................................................ ix

Preface ....................................................................... x

Chapter I  *Expanding Astute Revelations* ................. 1

Chapter II  Instantaneous Freedom ......................... 6

Chapter III  *Awesome Revelations* ........................ 11

Chapter IV  *I am Free* ............................................. 16

Chapter V  *Peerless Seer* ........................................ 21

Chapter VI  Forthright Pioneer ............................... 27

Chapter VII  *Glistening Genius* ............................... 31

Chapter VIII  *Rabble Rousing Innovation* ............... 35

Chapter IX  *Fear is Unrefined Wisdom* ................... 37

Chapter X  Adventurously Running to Fun ............ 43

Chapter XI  *Fearless Enterprising Audaciousness* .. 48

# Acknowledgements

A huge thank you goes out to my Mom and Dad who have passed for being my parents, and the work ethic and moral values they instilled in me. I understand I wasn't always the easiest child…

I thank my family and extended family: Nieces, Nephews, Aunts, Uncles, Cousins, Sisters and Brothers for being a part of my life.

I thank every one of my friends for being part of my life.

I thank Amy Lignor (www.thewritecompanion.com): published author, editor, ghostwriter, reviewer - who writes dynamic articles to expand your brand and enhance your bottom line.

I thank God, Mrs. Universe, the womb of unconditional love and enterprising energies, all people, spiritual ethers, metaphysical realms, physical playgrounds, mystical magical heavens of miracles, and all realized and unrealized sources in the cosmos, for opening the way to authorize and allow me to experience my life, *my way*.

I thank all my listeners and guests on *Cowboy Wisdom NLI Radio* at www.blogtalkradio.com/cwbywsdm.

I thank everybody who buys and reads to expand their life in a perfect way.

I am thankful for my life everyday in every way under grace in a perfect way.

***I love life and life loves me!***

# Author's Note

**Thank you for purchasing *Fear is My Friend***

*Expanding Astute Revelations!*

May life flow in lavish avalanches of affluent abundances now to eternity in the right way, in a loving way, under grace in a divine blessed way, and in divine order…**NOW**!

Robert A. Wilson

# Preface

Thank you for purchasing *Fear is My Friend*. *Fear is My Friend* opens the way for a dawning new understanding. Fears expand astute revelations opening canonized abilities to experience life in galvanizing gusto in a divine, blessed way. *Fear is My Friend* is written in the first person, so when you read this book, read as if *you've* written it.

As you read *Fear is My Friend* read it out-loud for the highest life-expanding experience. Allow the words to energize your vision, opening your heart and spurring your grit 'get up and go' and opening your conscious mind to see your visions on the horizon by realizing your talents and electrifying your intuitive wit to see the world as an opulent opportunity.

(To begin…)

Authorize and allow my enterprising ears to open, my eyes to see the visions on the horizon, and experience my heart's delight to be the 'white light' of rainbow enlightenment, unleashing my entrepreneurial effrontery. *Fear is my Friend* unlocks my blocks to feel my colossal success flow to me; it sanctions me to touch my cascading cash-flow and authorizes me to smell my oceans wealth and fill my day-to-day experiences by tasting the filet mignon of triumph. I will hear my winds of wisdom, listen to the universes with keen-witted wit, instantly witnessing the revelation of my very own "Life of Riley" to eternity.

Allow my visions to expand today and every day in every way with **Fear is My Friend!**

# Chapter I
## *Expanding Astute Revelations*

*Fear is my friend*…opening my heart, eyes, spirit, chakras, body, cells and mind; fear edifies, admitting real first-truths and expanding astute revelations.

My fears are emotional energy in my internal landscape that broaden my boldness, inaugurating rainbow brilliance to embrace the innate canniness that I encompass, *except* when I overlook the emotional charge of my fears.

With that, I am instantly in donnybrook in my inner identity, instigating my termite of turmoil into raising cane because I am locked and blocked in living the insane of the same; as I am stuck in the mundane because I wailed in fail, unwilling to book the look of wealth and success.

Therefore, I now cherish my qualms to be calm, to famously book the look of wealth and success, releasing my titan of triumph with a new wave of peerless prudence. I instantly grasp with aspiring look to book my keenly focused eagle-eyed all-wise regality; to brilliantly broadcast:

***I am the student of my journey! I am the master of my destiny!***

I **am** the teacher of my own experiences to fathom my fears emotionally animate, real, insightful enlightenment - because my fears are my first expressive admiration of my *iron-will* to embark upon my journey. My journey is to fertilize my sagacity, to empathize that my fears are my friend which unties my thrill-seeking cowboy to realize I comprise the wise to live my dreams since I appreciate my dreams are alive and thriving. My dreams are driving me to unleash a new, vibrant vision of me dancing my 'Divine celebration,' seeing me walk out of my cave into Disneyland as I expand my sand to understand that *everything* in life is a mystery of unrefined wisdom.

So now: I engage, expand, energize, and bring forth enterprise within my skin to experience life with gallivanting gallantry by unsheathing my galvanizing gusto.

**So now you and I go on a journey of,** Fear is My Friend.

First of all I recognize fear as energized, animated resolve, showing me my apprehensiveness in engaging in my dreams, so now my dreams dare me to expand auspiciously…magnifying success.

*How will I be jazzed to expand all my fears into my new sharp-witted friends, energizing animated richness in my inner landscape?*

To best comprehend, I am now in the 'flow of the go' when I let go of smearing my fears as falsified experiences. Actualizing real events in my inner landscape enables me to unlock a new consciousness that fears enflame - artificial reminders of events that never happened - only as fantasy entrapping acetic rancor.

Actual-eyes immature malice drops the anchor freezing me inside emotional laziness, rusting my internal trust to distrust my instinctive abilities, factiously etching asinine reservations in the subconscious scenery. I now appreciate my frank, edifying astuteness *realizing fear is unrefined wisdom* defining my charismatic character. The realization unsheathes my stouthearted decree, morally displaying that I am a fiercely eager beaver assertively releasing false evidence, erasing real trickeries, now liberating all fears as a fairytale embeds a unique apologue recognition, unrestricting a fabulous enchantment, and arousing my revered prudence to be the prudent student to triumph.

Sanctioning my stellar stalwart to disengage fear clears my inner landscape in order to *dispel fear from raising hell* being the ultimate excuse to provoke and invoke fault with everything except me, caustically causing guilt trips and uselessly intensifying lies of self-sabotaging disloyalty to me and my dreams. So now: I disallow and disband my fears from now to eternity. Disenabling them from encoding angst-ridden reservations un-hampers my scampering sage; telecasting new prophesizing phenomenon unseals the real deal…panic is my pal, authentically, natural, instinctual communiqué in my core countryside.

As I now comprehend that *fear is my friend*, escalating absolute renderings are freed; real, state-of-the-art endeavors resoundingly nurture determination to see the realness in fears. Fears either entice me to throw rice at my wedding of marrying my fears as my avant-garde partner, to gallantly charge into the 'wild blue yonder' with; a forthright, entrepreneurial affinity that rockets my inventiveness into a forward-looking enterprise, appreciating my robust currency streams. OR, it makes me ask if I should sink into the fink of goading myself into being a fanatic, pandering to my inner terror, slandering everything and everybody in the world; walking with head down as a loony, panicked fanatic, attacking my capabilities and stopping me in my tracks because I fall back into the mode of:

**_I lack the will to see my worries as a scurrying fiery exponent._**

An exponent actuating rebellion in overthrowing my pouting doubts, staunchly sanctioned to pull the trigger, shooting my vim and vigor of brainy bullets and bona-fide innovative clout to undoubtedly 'shout open' the gate to my *wonderful world of wisdom* which authorized me to see that *I entail a whale of impeccable liveliness* to revolutionize my life! Revolutionize my existence into a glowing world of galvanizing gusto, with omnipotent wisdom that invokes folks to let go of the right to 'dilly-dally pity-parties.'

That enticed dramatized trauma embedding frenetic frenzies, ingraining fears to forever terrorize my life, undid the lid and allowed me to open my eyes to see that, fear is a *bogus worrywart kidnapper* snatching my ideas. This unlocks this new smartness: <u>Fears are nothing more than thieves and frauds</u>.

Fears seen as encoding animosity and ruining my will is the fallacy of fear, because fear actually shows me I *lived through* the moment just to show - to make **me** see - that I can face every action revealed to me because I, quite frankly, engage audacious realness forthrightly, eavesdrop auspiciously, reach deep inside my internal lore to be self-assured that my 'newfound friend' expands astute reverence to communicate in prudent prophecy with the universal vista. I now real-'eyes' *fears are:*

*Self-inflicted, self-taught, self-generated, low-frequency vibrations that fanatically endanger the actual resolve within my own skin to be the Robber Baron of my world travels!*

# Chapter II
# Instantaneous Freedom

This authorizes me to understand that fears stem from ingrained figments, egotistically amplified and reek of failed effigies that only *appear* real because I chose to listen to other erroneous, asinine rhetoric. Rhetoric that fabricated every action because they wanted to ruin my dreams and went on gossiping to ruin my life by broadcasting their fearful, egotistical, asinine, benign bone-headedness that reeked and creaked with fermented, smug, snooty, arrogance.

*Their asinine rhetoric attempted to ruin another's dreams!*

They felt good about spewing their lies in society's rumor mill, nattering chatter-cooking with a look of fake-and-bake smugness that smeared their in-house fear by using blather-burping BS, ruining my life because egotistical maniacs invoked interior selfish terror and engendered all rumors about me to feed their own needy greediness and to sooth their egos because, subconsciously, **they feared me**. As they factiously thought they bullied me, in reality they terrified themselves by turning loose their own terrorized tyrant which was ingrained with their deep animosity, and rejected me in jealousy, invoking their 'four-flusher' emotions.

In frightful emotional remorse, they believed *everything* is fear, based on the falsely enclosed aching restlessness within their own hearts. Because **I** chose to unshackle my frontrunner by electrifying atomic reactor power within my skin, to illuminate all forced emotional acute repentance, I light up all darkness with love, light and dharma energy *just* because somebody decided to falsify episodes. They told the lie and made their ego feel emotionally happy, only to then adamantly regret every word they spewed!

***Lies have long legs and eternal memories; whereas the truth is <u>instantaneous</u> freedom!***

My fears are my gateway to experiencing 'Heaven on Earth,' allowing my first-class emotional animation, reinforcing my titan trust in my hallowed forte to saunter in sync. Distinctly sensing that the universal vista is my truss of white light, I gloriously 'mosey,' magnetizing the worldly ethers with my feisty effrontery, my autonomy reveling in potentate poise as I heartened my stainless trust in the universal truss of luminary sovereignty.

Correlating universal collaboration, intertwining my intuitive intentions from my heart to my eyes to my soul to the universe, authorizes me to stroll in sphere sapience - parading my undeniable *classy coolness* within my rebel readiness to step forth, out on the dance floor, to parlay my fears into organic ingenuity, magnetizing my intentions to the exosphere ethers, and showcasing the fact that I encompass the guts to fan my genius and radio-'eyes' my feisty, extreme, ardent rebelliousness within me. I seek out fears as friendly, enlightening, assertive rebel visions, showing me the path to fly unparalleled and unrivaled…

Rejoicing, communicating my first-rate entrepreneurial acumen and revving-up my lavish lucre to be the 'superstar' in my movie of sumptuous success in a willing, winning way, today and everyday, in *every* way, under the grace of God, Mrs. Universe, the womb of cascading cash flow, and me.

Opening my eyes to galvanize *all* my life's 'fun in the sun' festivities un-encumbers my steely courageousness. I am instantly cognizant of my kingly acumen to ferociously energize my auspicious rabble-rousing gunfighter's backbone. To witness my fears, as my fearless entourage audaciously rants and raves in waves of canny cleverness in a colossal way - boldly branding my canonized abilities to be my fighting entrepreneurial avatar, rising to *superstardom* to boom the zoom of blooming galactic sprightliness. Instantly I release my fierce forthrightness to engage actual 'real' life events with a farsighted enthralling acumen, revealing my excitement, unscrambling my front-runner emotional verve, and applauding my new resolute modernization in my soulful sensations.

This liberates me in my inner spree to feverishly enraptures my ardor - razor-sharp insight takes flight, idyllically illuminates my heart's delight to instantly live in unwavering farsighted emancipated autonomy, reveling in the calm, cool classiness that is me. So now: I am forever free, expansively amassing a 'royal flush' cash flow in the glow of my 'get up and go,' forthrightly emboldening my *awesome* rancher wit to fathom expansive affluence...

### *Releasing my core commodore to soar!*

As I 'wowed the world' with my divine light, I take flight. Featuring my feisty friskiness sanctions me to orbit in the mystery of risk - because *risk unhooks my tameness unlocks my gutsiness* - to proudly picture risk as my fanatic, enthusiastically standing humbly on my star epic fame - on my walk of preeminence, showcasing my unrestrained revolutionary gunfighter bravery…kicking me in the butt to strut my cutting-edge prudence. Fiercely energizing the amazing results and steadfastly admiring my internal fire as I eulogized awe-inspiring resilient 'statesman' sharpness.

To understand, I choose the way to engage my fears *as my friend* by expounding adroit realizations. This unfetters my glorious grandeur, unsheathes the kapish of my luminous flowing energy…acclaiming <u>reverence</u>. This un-kinks the links of my inherited fears as an enemy, as I swallowed a silly pill of illicit illusion that was my innermost, polarizing pollution that created my inbred dread of *taking action on my dreams*, as I instantly cut the threads of the dread, untangling inborn thinking, undoing the woo by saying:

### *How do you do!*

To my "ahead of its time" shrewdness, to savor an unwavering boldness. I independently authenticate my fears as my sassy, suave friend, rather than an enemy lying in wait within. This empowers me to enfold and behold my *fears as my new-fangled confidence.*

### *My fears are my internal fertile call to action!*

They unshackle my brand-new credence which allows me now to reap a lavish harvest of copious cornucopia from **all** sources in the universe in **all** forms; epitomizing affluence, relishing and embellishing my life today and *every* day as a glorious adventure. With commodore confidence, I freshened my ecstasy, highlighting my escapades and amplified my royal dignity in my heart, as I candidly befriended my fantastic, enthusiastic, emotional augury rebel to

**let go of fearing the unknown.** I unblock a cockiness, untangling firsthand experiences and admonishing repugnant residue that I just **had** to know *everything* and live in the known - realizing everything I know and *have* known stole my dreams.

*This is now gone…yesterday's dawn.*

# Chapter III
## *Awesome Revelations*

As I graciously galvanize full-fledged effrontery energies, accruing mind-boggling repercussions of splendid accomplishment, lauding a fulsome harvest fully entrenching awesome revelations - focusing on residing inside my desired bounteous bounty. Because I comprise stalwart supremacy to blatantly financially engage in my aspirations; to recognize the au fait in my novel sagaciousness…

Lionizes my omnipotent oracle to be instantly utilized, unswervingly employing my innermost sage to listen to my fears' query - the fear finding *every* apprehensive restless concern. I speak to the emotionally-charged impression by gently finessing my emotional energy from anxiety into a forthrightness, energizing my astute rabble-rousing soothsayer to philosophize and *mesmerize the wise* out there in the world into a new-fangled way to tantalize and tone triumph in folks hearts. I stand for beautification in the 'wow of now' to frankly expose adamant *respect for myself*, to fearlessly exude appreciation regarding other people's feelings and emotions. Because I now understand my fierce, extreme, ardent respect, I show myself to people in my aura, when I freely enjoy appreciating showing my respect for all people in the fame and fortune way.

To see all my intuitive adventures as a fertile energy; aggrandizing radical, spine-tingling, opulent outcomes, thrills my heroic heroism of my 'ism' to say I stimulate magnificent significance in my core - letting soar my finessing ferociousness. This strengthens my fortitude, expands astute, rambunctious, spiritual serenity to feel free, un-cluttering my ardent spirit and setting free my far-reaching ingenuity to open a conduit of fantasy.

## *Exhilarating!*

Articulating rhythmic capitalistic courage, making mountains of money while having fun, presenting my groundbreaking exhibitions to make life easy and effortless for all innovations, unpinning my winning, nascent notions of prosperity potions that undo my 'woo,' articulating my worldly opportunistic omnipotence to the universe.

To fantastically express a new rebellious eye-opening gutsiness that unties the *lies of fear as being an internal enemy* unburdens uncertainty and frees evolution, aspiring the retort of *I can*. I am unbound, profoundly broadcasting my innovative nudity. To give a free rein to my maharishi-mettle to flow, energizing aggrandizing, rapturous fierceness within me to love the preeminent pioneering me. I profusely exposed my brash frontiersman, emotional-'eyes'-zing aspiring razor-sharpness to superbly comprehend the world as a global gyration of pristine prosperity.

As I unchained my ingrained pain, emancipating my frontrunner entrepreneur, I astoundingly ran to the affluent abundance finish line of…

## *I won! I am done!*

I am having fun in this womb of mystery. Magically living in my kingdom of wisdom sanctions me to experience life as an appreciated champion - to feel real, fine, effusively esteemed and aristocratically rich.

Unrestricting my trailblazing titan to familiarize expansive affluence, relishing the guts to flourish, enjoying an alluring relaxed lifestyle inside my divine inheritance of ten million dollars - authorized and allowed me to finally be able to holler:

*I won my game of fame!*

With fearlessness and enhanced acute resoluteness to say Hey People! Look at my first-rate, enterprising, adroit, razor-sharpness to cruise as a muse on my seas of success; to brilliantly burst forth with enthused vigor. Allowing my savant sapience to be the 'flue of the do' endows and rouses my pioneering spirit. As I pass 'go,' fervidly entertaining animated rapture - futuristically enduring assuring rapport with my sired desires to fly high into the heavens - impressively loving each and every day henceforth by applauding robust richness in *every* phase of my life.

As I am a cosmopolitan debonair, flying bravely high through the cosmos, announcing I am a rabble-'eyes'-zing soothsayer expressing a zealous zing of wisdom - flinging enterprising ability and freeing my entrepreneurial artistry while I ravel in superb victory because…

*I let go of history to soar in mystery!*

As I confess I am free, expansively aggrandizing my 'real life' experiences, I am fancying each ambitious, red-hot, innovative idea that fluidly enters my awareness, resolutely freeing evolution-'eyes'-zing astute Rocky Mountain grandness!

I fluently express ardent rarity, daring my Fremont explorer who adventurously rides the rodeo, finishing first, emotionally energized, audaciously roping the winds of wisdom to ride the tide of plush prosperity.

Because I choose to free *every* astute revelation in my core décor to soar through the door, I am *forever* expanding the acumen-'eyes'-zing rallying point in my mind's eye to unleash my undaunted utopian forthright focus. Enhancing the dance of my aplomb, regal fluency, bestows me to proclaim the fame within me - to see the light of my savvy shrewdness in my fears, enriching atomic radioactive intuition to be the ignition of life!

My inventive vista idyllically illuminates farsighted entrancing visions, freelancing embolden, animated, royal rococo, let's go whooshes' my whizzing zeal on to the galaxy expressway, allowing me to voice:

### *Let's play today!*

I fluently emblazon amazing roads of cosmic cornucopia to experience nomadic nirvana. The intergalactic thoroughfares authorized and allowed me to go from 'rags to riches,' to walk my talk on my brilliant pathway paved in gold bars, energizing free-for-all, enthralling robust trust in my fountain of endless assiduous abilities and clearing the way for my 'rags to riches movie' to be flawlessly experienced and appreciated in my mystic eye.

This allows money to shoot out from *all* sources in the universe, mirroring the grand stream of steam that erupts from Old Faithful. The money flows fast and furious, enamoring abundance and releasing a universal cash flow by filling my prosperity accounts - like a treasure trove of vapor stored beneath the earth - as my gushing cash flow from the capitalistic cosmos streams to me in a bountiful blessed way that mimics Old Faithful's gushing steam.

As I admire my limitless resounding cash flow to glow in a golden embolden way, I love to say in a brazen bold way:

# Chapter IV
## *I am Free*

*I AM FREE!*

<u>Because</u> I opened my Wonderful World of Disney-decree in a wild, wonderful way to flourish, experiencing avalanches of rich serenity. I unhitched my valiant vigor. I undid the buzz, release-*sing* my freeway facilitator and emancipating my artistic Rembrandt talent dauntlessly daring me to say:

*"Hey! I won my game of life!*

**All** because I expanded my *fears into being my omnipotent oracle-'eyes'-zing friends*, energizing acute, radical, iron-will to birth my sired desires in the universal vista! As I told the world - I told **you** - in a bold way. I triumphed in the journey of worldwide wealth and across-the-board success because my uncertainties are now my *family*.

As I experience my sired desires today and *every* day in free-flowing, enterprising amazement, ratifying my real, audacious, tantalizing, innovative, forthright 'yeah'-zing inventor. I nurtured genius and floated on cloud nine because I look so fabulously fine while embracing rambunctious 'rock-n-roll' fame, enamoring arousing resources as I now understand fears are my first emotional action that reached my conscious mind from my subliminal landscape.

With this new understanding, *fears become my friends*, fearlessly espousals a rigid rebar backbone to stand up to my ingrained fears of fraudulent evilness. Acting self-centered righteous had me falsely believing my apprehensions were trying to protect, instead they stopped me cold. So now: all my suspicions are gone, like a new big-city center boom as I now recognize my fears - exposed appalling responses from previous experiences that I encountered in my daily life. I now compassionately appreciate my trepidations for budding new boldness in my daily adventures.

I am grateful *my fears are my friends*, expanding astute relations, opening my financial, enterprising awareness, revolutionizing my firsthand enlightenment. I realize I am living my 'Life of Riley' in galvanizing gusto today and *every* day, in every way under grace, in a lush, plush way, and in Divine Order…

### *NOW!*

Fears are 'worry wart wounds.' However, when expanded into new paradigms, wounds become wisdom - opening an undaunted fresh determination and saying:

**YES!** *to Colossal Success!*

Fears are ingrained pain of my fiery, egotistical arrogance; rim-firing old hurts that bring up deep emotional drama that flat out traumatizes me because of my old adage fears that are nothing but false evidence - only appearing to be real. That old adage is the plow of disallowing my entrepreneurial emotional landscape from expanding out, through and beyond the field of competition.

Egotistical arrogance provokes my fears, conceitedly invokes me to be in competition with **everything** caustically enraging my fear of - *What I*

*Know* - isn't enough. Other people know more than I and, "What are they saying about me?" just causes chaotic fear which is then used by society, friends, family and, oh yeah...employers. Fears are a society's and corporation's way of using your fears to free-lance their egotistical arrogance, ruining my dreams to push forth their agenda. Fears are forthright, emotional, astuteness, robustness.

Instead...I bowed down to my old die-hard way. I permitted my pigheadedness to fetidly entice, agitate and recite my old ways of responding to every given situation. How will you feel to be released from all unresolved hurt from fear, egotistical arrogance ruining your dreams? Because **my** fears are **mine** to explore, to expand my courage, wisdom and will to live **my** desired experiences.

Fears have been ingrained by history. So how are my fears figments exaggerating egotistical arrogance, raging inside me from situations in my life that are like a bad movie that just keeps running over and over? How are my fears actually my egotistical arrogance berating me?

When I expanded to understand that fears are the fallacies of egotistical arrogance reeking with expectations, want, need and greed...I let go of my peevishness. Amazingly I opened up to my fears, enabling an astonishingly real friendship, emancipating astute rebellious ideas to experience financial windfalls that I receive from **all** sources in the cosmos.

That movie is done and gone like a blown-up Tomahawk missile. **Now** I choose to unbolt the dolt of my horrors, unlock my lightning bolt colt, publishing my soothsayer foresight, expediting ambitious, rip-roaring good times in **all** phases of my life! Now I sit in first-class entranced affluence raving by the way I wonderfully foster effrontery ardent revelations.

Dauntlessly unmask my sharp-witted awareness valiantly opened me out to realize that fears are ingrained imprints in the subliminal landscape, captured in the cells of my body and DNA. This keeps me stuck at the buffet of fear, growing overweight while waiting to open the gate, as my date with procrastination baits me into foolish follicles of my diabolical dreads of being fed a line of burping BS, to be a follower of society's raining mundane.

I get 'everything for nothing' is the definition of being at the buffet of fear. Now my date with procrastination has reached its final destination; my procrastination and eating at the buffet of fear is forever expelled to hell - burned into admonishment - rebuked and duked like yesterday's desert rain as I choose to go on a diet, daring intrepid enterprising tenaciousness to riot inside *au fit grit* unfastens my crafty wit to **see**. My fears were utilized to keep me safe at one moment in time, but I immediately erased this encased enigma; I uncased my racy foresight, exhilarating my prizewinning entrepreneurial adeptness, ratifying my innate I am great throughout the galaxy illuminates my riveting gallivanting genius!

### *I salute my genuine gallantry!*

I am instantly free, expanding audacious revelations that I dauntlessly desire to feverishly escalate, adventurously revolutionizing my new untaught novelty to sharply thrill my visionary scenery. As I instantly un-impede my stampeding un-afraid parading wisdom, as it is unleashed I emanate a beaming brilliant 'buzz brashly unveiling a zinging zeal.' Launches a dynamic new paradigm, 'fear,' expounds astounding Reiki enlightenment, and sanctions me to say ***goodbye*** to fears that uselessly fueled egotistical arrogance that ridiculed me - ruined my high-tech philosophies.

# Chapter V
## *Peerless Seer*

When I choose to let go of thinking fear is false evidence artfully appearing real, I expand through-out and beyond my fears as I feistily empower alert revelations. Unveils new-fangled shrewdness unbinds my sublime mind to daringly grasp forthright emotional audacity, realizing I unwound my award-winning-wise to abound and astound the world by verbalizing my fears. I elaborate, collaborate and fluidize astute, exulting reverberating fortitude, emotionally amplifying razor-sharp focus an electrifying astronomical results, fascinating every aspiring notion in my inner landscape.

To familiarize, energize and aggrandize, I forthrightly raise the financial value of my effervescent acuteness, rousting out new prospering frontiers, entrancing amazing, riveting, panorama percipience; flashing enthusiastic awesome resources, and fabulously exciting astounding rhapsody in **every** featured episode of my amazing rapturous romp through life.

*I amass regal wealth today and every day!*

This new paradigm, 'fear,' is the first emotional audacious response to realizing new fortunes, emblazing astounding relaxation from my newfound exuberance. As I authentically retire from fear being my inner termite, "I am right" and the world is mired in wrong, and fear retires from being an instigator of falsehoods etching anemic resentment. Gone from all facets of my life instantly, I heartily do it my way in fun, ravishing my enlivened, amazing, rapturous nirvana to experience…

### *Heaven on Earth Panache…by gosh!*

I instantly unsheathed my bold brio and cognized my fears, enabling ardent respect that fantastically enlightens autonomous reverence that opens the way for me to distinguish my fears. I expose acute resourceful fearlessness by exhuming autonomous, revolutionizing omnipotence to understand, and be the vulnerable unconquerable and say "I am open!" Authentically audacious I am in exposing my *fears as my friend* -exposing authentic realizations about myself, as I faultlessly energize amazing results as I summersault through the air, flourishing effusive affluence and reveling in my opulent opulence. This opens the way for me to grasp the fact that my fears are nay saying follower's - extremely active reactionary retorts to former experiences that only *appear realistic to my unconscious mind* controlling my conscious mind. My subconscious images feature ingrained anonymous reactions to uncertainty. Fear is simply an illusion of delusional beliefs - of previous imprints activated from my daily life in the now.

As I unchain the pain of change from past experiences, these events are now gone like the Pony Express, and I uncover a fast breaking, empire-building, altruistic freedom. I fly high and free liberating my famous eagle-eyed animated Robin Hood, expanding the world into wealth and success by exposing fears for what they really are: *unrefined wisdom*. I own the red hot burning desire to fire-up emotional acuity, revving up my cascading cash flow in a bountiful blissful way.

Unbridling this new paradigm, I choose to soar like Thor. Unrestrained, my roving peerless seer with a fearless ennobling astute resolve to 'see!' I now understand fears are my frontrunner emotions that actually reveal raw, unrefined wisdom to be experienced in my new kingdom of farseeing effervescent artistry; revolutionizing racy *joie de vivre*, rounding the bends of success like a Kentucky Derby winner, communicating a far-reaching essence and alluring royal stateliness as I unwind and adore lavish avalanches of marvelous miracles **now**. As I watch me sashay down a road of royal riches, I sing with a debonair zing:

***"Hooray for me!"***

As I am THE superstar avatar starring in my boisterous adventurous rags to riches movie as I frolic, divulging my enchanted avant-garde rabble-rousing vanguard, bluntly baring my savant sassiness to say, "I am a **great** potentate with grit to gyrate my chakras to the right," as I magnetize the universal airwaves. With my free-spirit enflamed autonomy - riveting sovereign sagacious omnipotence - and visual-'eyes'-zing endearing, revered, empirical, inventive grandeur as my savvy philosopher expresses **hooray to all** that gives it their all every day.

When I choose to listen to my fears, they encompass insight to open forthright emblazing acumen by revving up my titan of triumphant, to unlock the lock and remove the blocks of my fears that fostered egregious, terrible recall for my reactions to the situations in my conscious mind.

Choosing to listen allows me to undo my fabricated 'egg-on-my-face' calamities, regretting my reactions from my first erroneous adamant recall of my moldy old patterns in my sublime scenery. I used to feverishly enfeeble by antagonizing and refusing to listen in order to see a better way to live my life in the physical world. This chaos caused my faulty egotist alienating retorts that had me living as a panicked fanatic sinking like the *Titanic*, simply because I refused to realize that I was a faceless, enraged, angry, reactionary living in the attic of my subconscious mind.

These non-powers are **long gone**! I am liberated from all fears, because now I recognize fear as fortifying, exhilarating and articulating revelations that set me free in my divine extravaganza. This allowed me to stop instantly from smearing my foolish 'egotism acid reflux disease' into my intuitive imagination.

I instantly un-tethered my groundbreaking ingenuity to fantastically expand, authorizing real resolutions to every situation because I **choose** to expand out of Pandora's Box of self-denial paradox. This paradox of how I *had to be right*, sustained an inner fright and exploited my arrogant righteousness. This blight on my 'Divine' light is long gone and allows me to let go of my fears.

I boldly tell myself directly that I have gallantly matured out of the place where I patronized my frightful exchanges. Abolishing recluse reasons promptly opens the way for me to excuse defuse, releasing all fragmented excitement and announcing royal freedom in my core domain.

The personal inflammation of blame caused my internal fanatic to go into panic mode that bound my conscious mind. Unbinding my subliminal mind and un-damning the shame, frees my subconscious landscape and authorizes me to unhook the 'plow of disallow.' It fervently ennobles awesome respect for myself, lighting up my heart's delight and canon-'eyes'-zing my iron-will to unlatch the latch of the fears of forgiveness…

I instantly disengaged the lock to courageously communicate my preeminent prize of 'inner wise;' to bodaciously cognize *fear is my friend*, expanding astute revelations, fissuring old paradoxes, and releasing old patterns unmasked my adroit abilities to unleash my courtly curiosity - exploiting my bold brio to extravagantly *experience life with gusto*!

I, frankly, exalt the resolve ringing the chimes in my subliminal mind to unleash my frontrunner enchantment, alertly realizing my enterprising-wise to pluck my luck of farsighted eulogizing axioms, rocking my rock-n'-roll rococo get up and go spurring my forward-looking entrepreneur.

As my Yahweh opens the way for me to see that *I am a peerless seer who understands my fears*. Brazenly births my winds of wisdom unpins my winning wit - embellishing my 'give it hell get all done now' attitude - relishing my fears and energizing my altitude. Rousing my shark attack action, robustly rousts out my hot-blooded heart.

Full of stouthearted valor I defend my fiery enthrallments acumen-'eyes'-zing/revolution-'eyes'-zing breezes of brilliance, unbinding my mind to facilitate enterprising affluent real sensations. I plant my seeds of wisdom and engage my first energizing astute revelations by unhinging synergy of my spirited inquisitiveness.

I am fascinated by my ardent 'real-McCoy' gusty grit unearths the girth of my omnipotent open heart ardently allows wisdom to empower my ambitious, rabble-rousing inventive ideas, fertile-'eyes'-zing and embracing the link-up of my free-will to be thrilled by nu-**clear** clarification, my inner horror now charismatically charms my emotional relaxation, revving-up oratory reverence, speaking to the worries of the world in wisdom to *release people from their fears*.

# Chapter VI
# Forthright Pioneer

My infinite spirit is unfettered and authorizing me to:

**Give thanks for <u>my</u> freedom extending a hand up to all so they may embellish <u>their</u> freedoms!**

Enriching acuity revealing God, Mrs. Universe, the womb of enterprising energies - to folks like me, idyllically illuminating the fact that, *I am thee forthright pioneer*, exploiting actual real-life emotional events, engrossing frontrunner effrontery autonomy resoluteness, fabulously expanding adventures while riding the rodeo of life - roping fears and tying fears into enterprising wisdom.

I am instantly an emancipated avatar, realizing my famous effusive affluence and savoring my farsighted, enlightened, shrewd fruitfulness in every facet of my life. My superstar avatar authorizes me to sail around the universal vista while singing my song:

*I instantly won my game of fame!*

When? Now!!! *How?* By fearlessly expanding adroit, rabble-rousing, dare-devil hardheadedness to **never** lambaste my internal landscape, or baste my ills to the cosmos as a wasted thought, or speak about a person in vainness. I let go of seeing 'creaky-weak' facets of the world of fascist false-isms, or allow internal or external sources to defeat or delete my Cowboy-up-pluck.

Because I ferociously evict egoistical arrogance from ridiculing me in any facet of my spirit voyage as I now synergize my fierce, emancipating, audacious rebel to unleash my dauntless savant to *speak freedom* - eulogizing awe-inspiring revered individualism of the fact:

***I see money flowing to me.***

As I perceive my feisty, vibrant Viking embellish my 'give-it-all nomadic spirit,' I empower my freeborn, enlightened, ardor resiliency by applauding my stubbornness to **never** quit unleashing my warrior titan. **That** highlights my frontiersman – opening the galaxy gate on my enterprising, adventurous rodeo-rider "get-up-n'-go" to showcase my *All-Around Buckle* of willingness to televise my trailblazer life-force!

I un-imprison my frolicking, electrifying, audacious righteousness, honorably maneuvering me through the fields of fears to setting free my enlivened, adrenaline-charged rancher to rope the gales of miracles - authorizing and allowing me to carouse and caress my magical magnificence of sumptuous success!

**Which is <u>mine</u> by Divine right!**

My fears evaporated, activating resplendence to dance foxtrot of omnipotence in my heart, body, chakras, soul, spirit, DNA - every cell of my enterprising spirit and mind. I understand the mind is behind the times so I now allow my heart to put forth a hand to bring my mind onto the dance floor to dance with my fears, forming a new budding romance of triumphant prominence. In a blessed way…in a heartfelt way…in the right way…in a loving way…under grace, in a picture perfect way…and - above all - in Divine order **now**.

I feel emotionally able to fathom my fears and expand amazing robust seeds of wisdom and understanding. I unbridle a new-fangled, forthright, emancipating acumen, revolution-'eyes'-zing a truly savvy warrior. My warrior sees life as an avatar adventure **today** and **every** day in an enlivened, enlightened way. I unlock a farsighted, energizing avatar by realizing my terrific toddler is my mature megastar magnet, lavishly revealing my never-ending avalanches of copious copiousness instantly in a ritzy, robust way!

I fantastically express awesome, rabble-rousing ideas, spurring people into action and opening the way for people to experience their free-flowing, eulogizing, affluent, *Life of Riley*, in a wealthy, award-winning way. *People are forever free* to see their awe-inspiring, regal, rich sapience that enriches the ethers of the universe with an:

### *I can expand fortitude!*

Promptly allows people to see a better way to experience their life **today** and **every** day in a magnanimous fine, effusive, affluent, remarkable way. People unleash a forever-expanding, affluent repertoire, authorizing and energizing their inner landscape to see the prosperous outcomes in their physical scenery.

As I vehemently cognize to real-'eyes' the words I speak, I brilliantly broaden my sagaciousness to express my visions to my subliminal mind to live my desired life **today** and **every** day in **every** way in a free flowing, effervescent, awesome, radiant way. Invigorating words fire-up expressions, awakening royal talent and mirroring the heart of a lion, the tenacity of a grizzly bear, and the gracefulness of a gazelle!

Letting 'fly' my farsighted, eagle-'eyes'-zed, aggrandizing, razzle-dazzle innovation to reside inside my zillionaire zenith articulating sassy sex appeal, I sit on my porch watching my sunset in ritzy luxury, *relishing every day of my life with grandeur while relaxing in a serene pristine way*!

Flying everywhere…astonishingly replying to life with wisdom, innovation, love and laughter in my free-decree - enlivening abundance and rejoicing in my will to *voice my intention*! My words bountifully broaden the wonderful world into spiritual, emotional, personal and financial wealth and success by using an open heart of serene opulence, and fissuring every apathetic, reclusive paradox in my inner countryside to free-lancing extraordinary adroitness and realizing my omniscient omnipotence.

### *Sail My Oceans of Wealth!*

Sail my oceans of wealth in a profuse, profound way while feeling ecstatically amazed as I reel in billion-dollar-bills from my depths of triumph, expressing how thrilled I am that *I showed the will to win by expanding my wisdom*! Invigorated newborn imagination unshackles farsighted, energizing abundance and real-'eyes'-zing my omnipotent inner peace.

# Chapter VII
## *Glistening Genius*

***Relish it!***

Fluently float effervescently, appeasing yourself by realizing the view of the world on cloud nine **today** and **every** day in a serene sensational way!

Golf on my fairways, extravagantly appreciating real life experiences - just like rich milk chocolate is to the taste buds - in a plush, pristine way!

Authorize me to understand that "fear is my friend," energizing adventurous, resplendent journeys in my daily life and opening out owlish wisdom to soar with the eagles, while focusing on my enterprising endeavors to walk the 'yellow brick road paved in gold bars' in a lush, plush way.

As I soar exponentially, ascending, radically liberating my savvy, unorthodox, utopian ways to colorfully fly into the heavens - unrestricting my forthright, extraordinary, astonishing, regal view, communicating my crystal clear vision of my fame and fortune - sanctioning me to uncover and discover my frontiersman eyesight by appraising my rivers of glistening genius and unleashing my warrior lore.

I mirror the mighty Bald Eagle surveying the landscape, soaring **so** unencumbered…much like an adherent rocketeer exploring the wilderness, photocopying the universe that exudes freedom, energizing acumen and relishing **every** second of my life in a wise, relaxing way!

As I boldly engage my visionary mountaineer majesticness, showcasing profound, enterprising, amazing, revolutionary inventions that enrich the lives of people allowing me to bask in the glow of prosperous affluence in an brightened, calm way.

Enlightening my foresight, edifying accomplishments regarding my intuitive abilities to listen and communicate in the moment. Therefore, I fearlessly and ardently respect others in a friendly, extraordinary, ardent, respectful way.

As I now unchain frank, effervescent, adroit, reverential willingness to step forth into my purpose in a fearless, expanding, adventurous reverence to bask in the sunshine of my revered freedom; to flawlessly embellish avalanches of 'Rolls Royce' riches in a luxurious way. I piquantly fuel expansive ardor, royally appreciating my plush, pristine prosperity, enriching the landscape by opening the universal scenery into amazing richness.

I see my foremost enthralling, abundant rococo stylishness and un-cage my free-lancing achievements, as I ravish my extravagant limelight - **forever** enjoying absolute relaxation on my mountaintop of spectacular splendor.

*I am victorious.*

Feeling enamored, appreciating resolution, liberating my forward-looking, empire-building, adroit rabble-rousing - unlocking my carousing frontier-enduring awesomeness with fire in my belly to finish **everything** amazingly grand!

My core clearness comes from saying, but undauntedly understanding, *I am fancy-free*, entrancing 'Abracadabra' as I reveal **real** magical outcomes. Because of the 'buzz' I am miracle-flowing, ever-expanding, aggrandizing richness in my heart, chakras, body, spirit, soul - **every** fiber of spiritual light - flying everywhere most ardently.

I now understand that 60% of **all** communication is nonverbal - freeing astuteness and realizing I encompass 60,000 thoughts and 85,000 emotions. This allows me to fantastically empathize authentic reverence to people I communicate with by watching their body language, which opens me out to keenly familiarize each action, respond to any situation, or a person who's speaking to me, with fruitful edifying acumen resolve.

I can unfasten effective, amazing, robust listening prowess to harmoniously hear what the other person is saying, as I watch his body language and calmly fathom emblazing, aggrandizing - **real** - serene words; appealing, free-flowing energy that adamantly rousts out my newborn intuitive shrewdness, as I opened out my counterparts innovative cleverness. Together we opened out a *Trendsetter* friendship, allowing our relationships to flow effervescently as I am emboldened to my robust trust in my abilities.

I fathom **every** affluent revelation, un-cinching the synergy of mystery of my magnificent Yahweh superstar who sagaciously shouts out extraordinary, robust *"Yes's!"* to my inner avant-garde. I finish **every** assignment, revealing my seas of success and sailing freely, enjoying and reveling in well-heeled accomplishment. I open my frills, empowering audacious, rabble-rousing, soothsayer quick-wittedness to amble out of my imaginative fluency, edifying animated results and opening my torrential money streams from **all** sources in the universe.

It is because *I choose* to fervently energize autonomous resolve to entertain my undaunted, urbane fame as I now foresee empyreal awesome rapture. I unbolt fearless, enterprising, astonishing representation of my inner sensation by fueling ardent revelations, and unbridling the flaming escalating fire of my resplendent desires.

My *superstar flair* expresses my dynamic flair at the world fair, flaunting my extraordinaire, pure debonair, resourcefulness to be the 'seer.' **Your** seer. As I am the forefather...ennobling astonishing robustness and un-tethering my talisman talent to fly galaxy high, in awe of my high-spirited rococo.

*"Here we go!"*

Yes...here **we** go! Into the wild blue yonder, floating ever so awesome, rollicking the frolicking, everlasting avatar as I ride with pride astride a fast epiphany. I inspire resonance by announcing that my prosperity accounts overflow with cascading cash flow that is revving up with lissome luxury, streaming sumptuous success, beaming my tithing - reoccurring day after day in my life.

# Chapter VIII
## *Rabble Rousing Innovation*

*This is a windfall*; a financial expansion astounding **real** luxury in my endowing arts and lighting up my heart to dart dreamy agility radicalism, tantalizing my gutsy gusto as I am fiery expanding adeptness rapidly broadcasting rainbow brilliance.

As I instantaneously revolutionize my frontline energies I amplify *resipsa-loquitur*, which means I speak for **me**, freeing, exhilarating, audacious, rabble-rousing, innovative ideas, featuring enterprising acuity and relishing a luxurious experience in *every* facet of my life. I unlock emotional feelings emerging, actualizing realization as I *fiercely* engage in activating rococo, heartfelt extravagance to sail feverishly expanding autonomous realism.

I unbridle 'Frontiersman' élan, awakening rich milk chocolate ideas by unbinding my artistic mind to fantastically electrify my intentions that enter my conscious scenery from my intuitive inner-landscape as unrefined wisdom flows effervescently applauding rambunctious imagination, as I feverishly expand unprocessed inventiveness into ambitious realizations that fears **are** emotional axioms replying.

The truth is flowing with fervent electric acuity, rousing my adventurous 'Rambo-Let's go!' frontiersman entrepreneur acuity, reverentially unsheathing a futuristic, expansive audacity, and revving up first-class élan in **every** plush, luxurious facet of my life in a *fearless, peerless* way.

## Robert A. Wilson

Fear is a false emotional attachment reeking delusional mayhem in the imaginative landscape creating frosty endless addictive roadblocks disavowing natural philosophies. To flood expressive animated reclusive tumultuous emotions transforming me into a hold-em fold-em effluent aggressive rash crash and burn internal turmoil is instantly foiled and sent away instantly unconstricting my fourth-dimension expansive ascending rectitude exciting a Fourth-of-July emancipating attitude revs-up my new attitude.

# Chapter IX
## *Fear is Unrefined Wisdom*

Fear is unrefined wisdom opening out fear is my friend expanding astute revelations unleashing my canonized abilities energizing my enterprising listening freeing my entrepreneurial wise igniting global omnipotence to glisten from my inner kingdom to experience life with galvanizing gusto unbridling my genius utopian tantalizing omniscient opulence in every facet of my life in a pristine prosperous way

Fear entices a 'frothing at the mouth' emotional aggression, ruining people's lives because they buy into the fear as a *forever* egotistical arrogance, resistant to witness their desired life, which is a fallacy; ingrained aggravation romanticized by society.

"Once you have a fear you have that fear for life," is a fragmented flight of fabrication, egocentrically antagonistic repulsion shying away from my inner grandeur. I now grasp the fact my fears are **me**, afflicting annoying repentance upon myself.

I fantasized being the underdog in my life experiences then riding in at the right moment to be the hero, but instead, I ended up in a frantic, egotistical, angry rampage; the world is against me in realness. Yet it was **me** against **me** my desired life, fighting with my fictitious, egotistical, arrogant rival just living for survival - hoping for a better life. "The world is against me," is why I am unsuccessful, which all my fears and worry are priggish poopy-poppycock is now down the drain like life - yesterday's bath water.

Immediately opens the way for me to step to the forefront of my fears, fantastically extending appreciation and relishing my fears as my friendly energies applaud **real** new wisdom, as it flows through me to the universe. I expand fame, fortune and quick-wittedness, opening people's eyes to see that their *fears are their friends* to comprehend. We are **all** friends to live in omnipotent peace today and every day, in every way, in a fearlessly endearing ardor, holding respect for each other in an idyllic friendly way and in Divine Order **now**.

This authorizes my pristine prosperity release to flow energetically, and audaciously ripens my frequent-flyer miles to soar through the universe like a superhero. I free everybody auspiciously, releasing newborn foresight, enlightening awesome 'Rock-n-Roll,' fluently enthralling my awe-inspiring river of prosperity and frolicking, enhancing, altruistic, rustic morality.

Fears falsely emit actual responses to a situation in my daily life. They are the first emotional assumptions reaching the conscious mind in a friendly encounter; attunes radar focus by enamoring astonishing results and prosperous passionate freedom, enticing abundant, resourceful love by unfastening my forthrightness. Emancipates astute replies to find *new* forward-facing, exalting awareness - resplendently unbinding flair - entertaining alert rapport with my inner fears while enabling audacity - reaping new wealth from wisdom, and expanding affluence by *loving today*!

I am instantly fortunate, endearing automatically, radioing festive entertainment by experiencing the thrills and frills by energizing aspiring realizations -

famously empowering audacious, rabble-rousing, full-blooded enchantment. Awakening maverick regality liberates my frontrunner, thrilling my iron will to be free-flowing by expanding and appreciating *real* life experiences!

Because I realize *my fears are my friends*, energizing affluence radically reaping the bounty of my gutsiness to face **every** act, recognizing **every** fear as a new gutsy 'friend' engaging my adroit, rebellious heart to see me - listen my way through my challenges rather than feel erroneous, apologizing respectfully for something *somebody else* said I did, which is a fib!

***Listening to the klutz - taking the blame for their shame - makes a self-demoralized putz.***

While being the klutz can change into a putz, in the sham of shame to express the 'fink of their think,' trying to use me as a crutch to smear their fears. This is the asinine, repugnant 'putz' way of over-thinking their faults, exposing admonished, redundant punditry as their fameless blame goes frantically cockeyed, looking to book a victim racketing up their doubts and etching their victim-**I**-tice, egotistical brat within - then are bewildered as to why there life goes awry. They try to pin their painful vainness upon me and they are now crying, because trying to fault **me** for **their** embarrassment does not suffice.

***Because say with a brazen boldness: the shame upon me is now gone.***

Rather than listening to flaming, blaming falsehoods ingraining affronting repercussions in the inner landscape - instead, I un-constrict my inner dignified grandeur by voicing my first emotional acumen, realizing I was listening 'in the moment,' while deep inside I realize they are pointing their finger at **me** for **their** reprehensible ways.

So now I am free, expanding acuity and reaping colossal treasures and championing being a titleholder. I confess to myself, facing my fears as unprocessed prophecy opens the way for my unlimited, free-flowing, expansive affluence; relishing my financial enterprising astuteness; rallying my inner financier as I enhance a reveling cosmopolitan champion; taking off my 'fake and bake' smug duds of, "I am better than others." Smarter than others.

Backstabbing or belligerently blathering about others obstructed and sealed me in frivolous egotism, anarchist repugnancy of fear, distress and worry, smearing doom and gloom in my 'think outside box paradox.' I **now** understand *any* box is a paradox, and this untangles my cowboy-up wrangler to *maturely* ramble through life in a sphere of sapience, unbolting my bold, fearless, entrepreneurial ardor to roar and soar into the wild blue yonder of lavish lucre and valiant victory - in an energizing enterprising way.

### *When I look in my mirror my eyes see a prophesizing prophet.*

I am prophesizing wealth, winning *every* day by appreciating love and tantalizing hallowed forthrightness and engrossing avatar richness. My DNA opens this parvenu premise and my DNA stands tall, declaring my *Natural Abilities*; canonizing <u>fierce farsighted</u> entrepreneurial ambition and <u>rearing fearless</u>, enterprising assiduousness - rousting out - releasing forthright, enamoring acuity and relishing the freeing of *every* atom of my spiritual energy. I am to rally my frontier 'essence,' aggrandizing racy: "I can do the woo exalting whimsical omniscient omnificence!" by unthawing my flaming, endearing assiduous, spreading "Wow!" in my inner décor.

I now understand that "Wow!" is wisdom; optimizing wealth and un-tethering my famous effrontery to glide and slide in my mystery of wisdom optimizing omnipotence. I face each anxiety by reaching deep into my inner landscape to look into my 'face of fear' that's my brand-new friend, expanding astute, revolutionary wisdom to unleash my canonized abilities.

## **The Light of My Dauntless Desires**!

I am a fantastic, noble, acute rebel that fissures every angry response and opens the way for me to play in the light of my dauntless desires. I can expand my fearless, endearing, acute resolve to say, "Hey!" to the man I am here today to play.

***I am living in my luminary light, loving my financial freedom flight, savoring my glorious life!***

In freedom, I am enjoying affability as I relax on my bountiful beaches of pristine prosperity, because I *choose* to frankly embellish almighty ripeness in my judicious maturity.

At every 'first-light' I engender allegiance, rendering flamboyant, eloquent ambiance by ratifying my fluidity, emitting awe-inspiring, radiant feistiness, effusively amplifying regal riches. To forever and always rise to the challenge in raring-daring ways in *every* way and in *all* ways, is the objective. To play today for my "hooray" faultlessly, enamors all-powerful realism from my heart by understanding the 'ism' of *realism*. I serve mankind by igniting servitude, miraculously initiating self-assured maharishi idioms as I dauntlessly expound innovative oracle mantras augmenting colorful charisma in folk's hearts.

Saying *fear is my friend*, I expand dapper, astute revelations in my daily encounters, authorizing my foremost expressiveness to articulate renowned and profound in feisty, energetic, atomic reverence - detonating smart bombs of compelling cleverness as I repel the 'insane' of the same old, moldy paradox that fear is fallacy, entrenching aching repulsive life as I fantasize events, apathetically repelling my internal fortitude to allow my fears to factually embezzle affluence and rake me over coals.

# Chapter X
# Adventurously Running to Fun

Since I understand forging excuses, apologizing for ruining my life because I permitted and okayed my fears to be my free-loaders, entailing awful regret in my core décor because of the way **I** frequently was the ruse abusing **me** and excusing **me** from relishing **my** desired life. This is now in the category of non-existent 'has-been's' because they've never been only in constricting conceitedness" as strongly rocket my forthright, enterprising, avant-garde - rollicking my frolicking experiences and applauding my 'range boss' personality to be rough and ready to ride the open range and unbridle my rodeo rider orneriness. With rough and ready willpower as I empower the downpour showering the world with riches, common sense and dynamic health with *real* determination. I decree freed "OM," expressing avatar rancher wit grit and get to say:

***I shamelessly open fabulous endeavors, adventurously running to my fun in the sun.***

With these words I enjoy ardent relaxation, flexing excellent appeal and recalling my sapience to say it's okay to let go of anything I desire in my subliminal landscape. I *must* face each appearing reality with a forthright energy, activating rousing will from *every* acute, renowned flashing, expanding, and astounding righteousness. I am illuminated! Rowdy, euphoric animation; reverberating free-speech; enlightening awe-inspiring refined nobility - **all** of which allows me to walk fancy-free, applauding regal acumen to play in 'prime time.'

I chime the rhyme in my sublime limericks, singing my songs of audacious, outrageous victory as I embrace risks with a frisky, enriching, authentic, revered insight that unlocks my inner freedom - embracing amazing razor-sharp focus, exhilarating my ascending rocketeer's get-up-and-go!

I elaborate, celebrating my heart-smarts in the universal utopia as I zealously express <u>I am the peerless forerunner</u>! Enduring amazing, robust gusto while articulating fiery, astonishing regality unleashes endless lush, plush infinite streams of money.

The *'ism'* of realism is what **I** graciously receive, gratefully accept and compassionately appreciate - my over-the-top infinite supply of money today and **every** day in a loving luxurious way.

Final-*eyes*-zing enormous affluence by regally telling the universal utopia that <u>I am a self-assured monarch</u>! I am the frontiersman, expanding astute richness to showcase my inner being and flaunting my undaunted, forward-looking, endowing, adoring, roaring opportunities! My wise, apple-pie rowdiness combines with my prosperous landscape that firstly entrances articulate, reverential, hypnotizing **me** to be **free** - embellishing affectionate relaxation every day to expand my wisdom to enhance the freedom dance in the world.

As I now understand, dreams are daring, regal, energizing, audacious, magnanimous, stout-hearted clout - telecasting forthright enterprising abilities that rev up my wealth and success allowing me to confess the fact:

### *Fear enlivens adventurous resolution!*

This clarifies and illuminates my path of profuse prosperity. This opens the tantalizing harmony of life and shows that 'fathoming effusive affluence' *really* occurs when I let go doubt, and delete the fallacy that is embraced by society's ingrained poverty conscious, that enrages a caging again and again raining on my parade of prosperity. As I now realize **I** am the one raining on **my** parade of prosperity.

Fear…poverty consciousness, is boldly told to the populace by a stealth-controlled leadership to keep us weeping in our sublime mind; to keep us duped into thinking *everything* is and will be fine as long as **you** feel **you** belong in the fallacy of 'society falsified edification.' They adamantly deprive all *real* ability in the populace. As of this instant, I am the WD40 freeing *every* individual from *every* falsification. Eroding all ingrained pain that is instantly drained from all subliminal imprints now, as I set free feisty, enthusiastic, authentic, **real rowdy** cowboy get-up-and-go. Fear angers my audacious rancher whose wisdom to 'play in the frontier' with cowboy-up rowdy rodeo rider agility, to ride the winds of challenge, roping the mystery of wisdom that:

### *Fear is my friend!*

My passion is strong to open my courageous hero, to feel entrepreneurially awesome while rallying my spiritual 'seer' to fantastically engage, aspire, and revere sassy forthright spirit. I allow him to see, hear, smell, touch, and *feel* the 'prime time,' fascinated, enraptured and awestruck. I now authorize and allow myself to see *fear as a friend*, ingraining *real* enterprising-wise to feel emotionally audacious and render free-flowing energy by astutely rallying my rabble-rousing soothsayer 'seer' to walk fancy free.

I now comprehend *I am my best friend*, shaking hands with my newfound friend, and her/his name is FEAR! So I firmly shake hands with my new friend, FEAR THE III. Understanding I comprise the wise to see my inner sapience begins a raw, robust, energized, emotional outburst from ingrained imprints the conscious mind calls 'fear.' My subliminal calls it, keeping me safe in daily adventures as I now venture into the mystery of my fears and emancipate and activate my robust get-and-go. Unsheathing my internal frankness, I energize astro-metaphysical revelations, real-*eyes*-zing the **honest** *fear of life is listening to falsely expressed accusations*, revealing my crusty distrust of my frontiersman grit while shaking hands with my new way of experiencing life as my feisty frontiersman exudes emancipating audacity - rousting out the *thieves of my dreams that were renting my innovative talent for free!*

They were fermenting *every* acute reverie, setting me on my derriere in fear because I fragmented each animated revelry, emotional liveliness by unwinding my flawless empire-building august ranger, riding the range of utopia cornucopia. I update the slate. Society's 'political correctness' unlocked a new way of looking at fears as simple societal gossip, employing mundane blame in populace-conscious scenery. I furiously abash societal 'sheep-dom,' weeping in deep sorrow because I was *borrowing* wisdom from others falling in the fold of:

***I sold my soul to fit in with the fearful…***

I sold out to formulate, emulate and actuate the robbery of my own innovative inventiveness, drawing a line in the sand to stay inside the insane of the mundane, living vain pain that was further ingrained by a lying on the couch with a puckered lip as I tried to 'fit in' to the constant back-biting, fighting, egoistical ado by repeating every life event. I frothed at the mouth when encountering daily life because the daily encounter pushed a 'hot' button of panic. I was a fanatic, running away from the situation.

# Chapter XI
## *Fearless Enterprising Audaciousness*

As of now I fathom idioms arousing royal rich oracle, Yahweh, loving every situation with sharp-witted new frontrunner, superstar-talented individualism, relying on my judiciousness, engaging, gallant heart; illuminated spirit; and fresh, enterprising acuity. I am rollicking, as I frantically embalmed the awful response when it was time to step forth and enter an awe-inspiring *real* newness in my daily adventures. I admire my fearless enterprising audaciousness, realizing I am the *squire of my empire*, zinging my 'kingly zeal.'

To appeal to my subliminal mind, I chime the rhyme. I let go of my fears doing the 'pooh' in my own stew, so I evicted the fanatic that lived in my sublime attic who panicked in ruination rancor, that frivolously embarrassed my astute apparatus, and apathetically ran around like I ran in circles until I dropped, because *somebody* told me to crap in the corner of my round house and invoked the hoax of my fear. I believed if I said 'no' they would stop being my friend, as I now real-'eyes' my so-called friend pushed 'hot' buttons of fear, feebly entrenching ambiguous rogue untruths about them being my cohorts, mentors…friends. They falsely embedded an appalling, rickety self-esteem just to keep me weeping in the same mundane stew they swim in every day.

***My mundane stew is now gone like <u>yesterday's dawn</u>!***

This 'thanks' goes to me. However, all of this opened the way for a *new dawn* of dreams, aggrandizing wisdom and nurturing a new preeminent premise in my enterprising wise. It opened my prosperous eyes to relish and embellish the fact that distresses **are** my friends, intensifying smart, world-shattering phenomenon that I now forthrightly fathom. My effusive affluence is revving up. My 'ritzy glitzy' galvanizing gusto to experience the flow of my glowing over-the-top, floods of profuse profusion - today and *every* day - coming from the fact that *fear is my friend.*

I now understand **I** am the one that listens to fear, regardless of whether it is positive or negative. So, now **I** say this to me and the world!

***To know is to fear; to understand is to befriend my fears!***

Extracting astute resolution from my spiritual soothsayer-seer unleashes my idolized capabilities to foresee effective acuteness, rendering vibrant visions in my sublime mind to be victoriously felt - exciting, awe-struck realizations coercing my Teton zest in my intramural enthusiasm because I now **see** life with a sunlit wit, baring my free-will, enlivening astronomical resounding maturity, fostering embryonic animation, romancing my kiss-and-tell genuine genius to speak brilliantly. Marveling at me, I fearlessly stroll through my daily escapades naked - showcasing natural ability that kinetically epitomizes me, daring me to love living every day in the moment, exposing my natural born flair to ride the carnival rides at my universal fair because **I** am bodaciously-meshed money superstardom, hallowing emotional discernment in my worldly endeavors, forever exalting affluence as I rest - chillaxing on tropical beaches in lavish abundance in a bountiful blessed way.

I am the **only one** who can listen to fear negatively. Therefore, I revoke my rights to listen. Believing fears are falsified events activating responses, opens my 'out' to eavesdrop, acquiring resources from within me to respond with first-class elegance - authentically responding in a respectful, wise way. I now encompass a forthright effrontery, an ascertaining resolve to appreciate <u>me</u> because my fears exemplify admiration, revealing my stout-hearted grit to step forth and face the challenge with vanguard wisdom - unraveling a parvenu paradigm that <u>I</u> choose to.

Now I listen to *fear as my friend*, energizing astute realizations. <u>Fear is wealth</u>. It is a wisdom all its own that expands affluence and teaches to love today harmoniously, and experience the "Life of Riley" in zealous zest in a rich, regal way.

I love this day as I love life, because I now understand that *fears are my friend* and the *only* one who can listen to play the way I dauntlessly desire is **me**. I now grasp with class to utilize the wise of my fears; I choose to see my fears encompassed within amazingly rich, white light.

So I am now **free**, enjoying my inner spiritual spree in a fun loving way! Loving fear as my unrefined wisdom, expanding my intuitive innovation, because I engage in my daily adventure with feisty frontiersman effrontery astuteness, revolutionizing new canonized abilities today and **every** day in a forthright **freeway**, and in divine order…**NOW**!

# ABOUT THE AUTHOR

## Robert A. Wilson

I hope you enjoyed, ***Fear is My Friend***. I am Robert Wilson, NLP Practitioner, Hypnotherapist, Past Regression Specialist, Reiki Master, Radio Show Host, Parts Integration and Time Line Coach.

*Cowboy Wisdom NLI Radio* is on Tuesday and Thursday at 8PM Eastern/5PM Pacific and has reached out to listeners. *Cowboy Wisdom* in known to open people's eyes so they see their talent and engage in their intrepid intentions instantly.

*Cowboy Wisdom Innovation Coaching* opens

your enterprising listening to unmask your entrepreneurial wise and unleash your canonized abilities so you see **all** the opulent opportunities to experience your copious outcomes in galvanizing gusto - now to eternity.

*Cowboy Wisdom Innovation Coaching* shows you how to embark on your own journey to energize your financial, spiritual, personal and emotional sovereignty by galvanizing brand new subliminal blueprints that steer you **out** of the world of confusion and **into** the world of wisdom, in order to unleash your entrepreneurial talents. It electrifies your choices and bonds your day to day encounters with your pioneering genius that allows you to real-'eyes' your highest results. By unifying your everyday life and your desired life, you unlock freshly minted understanding to reveal your boundless financial, personal, spiritual and emotional independence in **all** facets of your life, authorizing you to experience your life's purpose and open the gates to your copious cornucopia!

Robert A. Wilson

www.cowboy-wisdom.com

rob@cowboy-wisdom.com

cwbywsdm@gmail.com

**Skype:** cwby.wsdm

Robert A. Wilson

# A SPECIAL THANK YOU TO YOU!

On behalf of everyone at Freedom Of Speech Publishing, thank you for choosing Fear is My Friend for your reading enjoyment.

As an added bonus and special thank you, for purchasing Fear is My Friend, you can enjoy discounts and special promotions on other Freedom of Speech Publishing products. Visit www.freedomeofspeech.com/vip to learn more.

We are committed to providing you with the highest level of customer satisfaction possible. If for any reason you have questions or comments, we are delighted to hear from you. Email us at cs@freedomofspeechpublishing.com or visit our website at: http://freedomofspeechpublishing.com/contact-us-2/.

If you enjoyed Fear is My Friend, visit www.freedomofspeechpublishing.com for a list of similar books or upcoming books.

Again, thank you for your patronage. We look forward to providing you more entertainment in the future.

## Fear is My Friend
## By Robert A. Wilson

For more books like this one, visit Robert A. Wilson's website at:
http://cowboy-wisdom.com/
2012 copyright by Freedom of Speech Publishing, Inc. All rights reserved. No part of this book may be reproduced, distributed, or transmitted in any form or by any means, without permission in writing from the publisher.

Printed in the United States of America
The publisher offers discounts on this book when ordered in bulk quantities. For more information, contact Sales Department, Phone 815-290-9605, Email:
sales@FreedomOfSpeechPublishing.com

Product and company names mentioned herein are the trademarks or registered trademarks of their respective owners.

Freedom of Speech Publishing, Leawood KS, 66224
www.FreedomOfSpeechPublishing.com
ISBN: 1938634284
ISBN-13: 978-1-938634-28-4

www.ingramcontent.com/pod-product-compliance
Lightning Source LLC
Chambersburg PA
CBHW071416040426
42444CB00009B/2273